TOOLS

The tools necessary to accomplish the decorating illustrated in this book are quite basic. The techniques used are those used in professional decorating to achieve the highest quality results in the shortest time.

TOOLS:
1. **SCISSORS**– Should be high quality, sharp - about 3 or 4 inches of blade length.

2. **DECORATING TRIANGLES**– Due to the many different colors and tube sizes needed to do good quality figure piping, it is usually more practical to use decorating papers rather than canvas or plastic cones for this type of decorating.

3. **METAL SPATULAS**– I prefer spatulas with blades about 1 inch wide and about 6 inches long.

4. **PASTE FOOD COLORS**– Have a good selection on hand.

5. **METAL DECORATING TIPS– (optional)** A method of piping many professional decorators use is simply to cut off the tip of the paper decorating cone and use the resulting opening as the decorating tip. Care must be taken, however, when using this method to ensure the tip is cut off cleanly, squarely, and to the correct size. This is not as difficult as it sounds and will give beautiful results with good speed if done correctly.

   If you find you have difficulty achieving good results using this method, you may want to use the commercially available metal tips.

Though it is usually unnecessary to use a palette knife or artists brushes to smooth or detail the small figures we make for cupcake tops, there is, nevertheless, a time they may come in handy for these small designs. These tools are often needed, however, when piping these figures in a larger size. They can be of great help if any shaping or smoothing is necessary.

A **set** of artists' tools consisting of four high quality brushes and a palette knife (ideal for cake decorating purposes) is available from **Winbeckler Enterprises.**

Also available is a pattern book containing 21 of the most popular cartoon patterns and useful designs ever assembled. *"Fun To Use Cake Decorating Patterns"* also includes instructions on how to make stencils; and tips on how to use these patterns to aid in drawing or piping on cakes.

Winbeckler Enterprises welcomes your comments concerning this book or subjects you would like to see in future books.

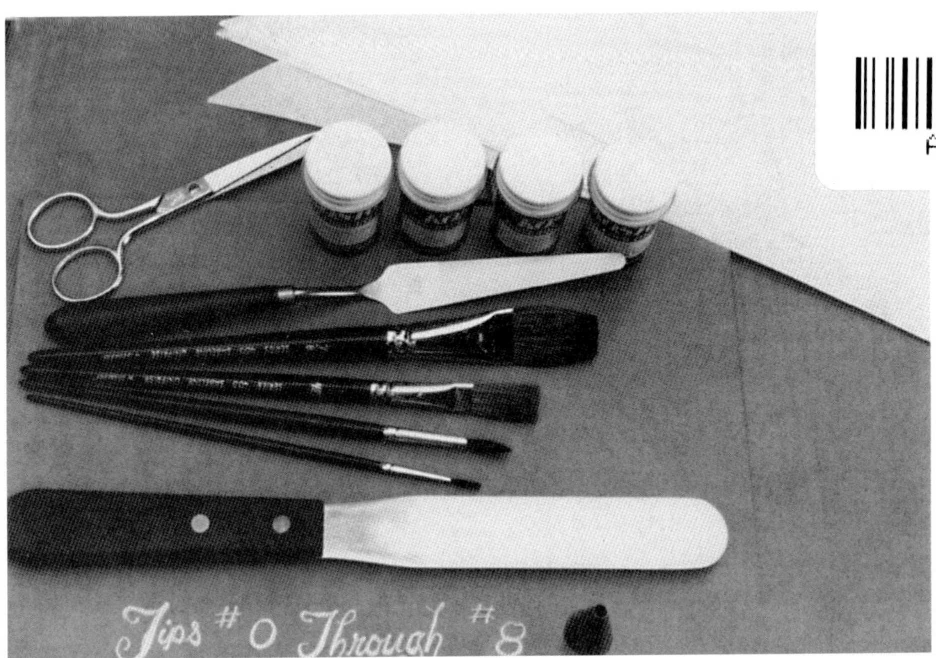

This design is among the most popular to ever grace the top of a cupcake. It seems that just about everyone loves frogs, at least the ones made of icing. But alas, all frog cake decorations are not created equal. The fact that a cupcake top affords us only limited space to work with should not limit us to dull, lifeless designs. Though cupcake decorations must be fairly simple, there is no reason they cannot be crisp and alive. Much of this "life" is achieved by using vivid colors and tubes of a proper size. It is especially important to use a small opening or tip when drawing on the fine detail of the faces.

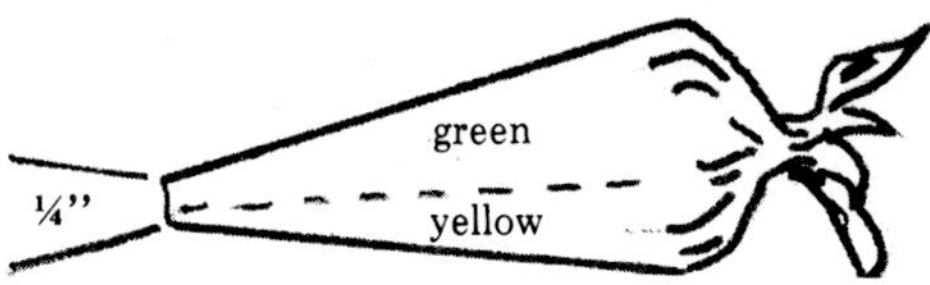

To fill the tube. Stripe one side of the tube with yellow icing. Then fill with green.

Note: When piping the frog, hold the tube so the yellow is at the front. The frog will then have a yellow tummy!

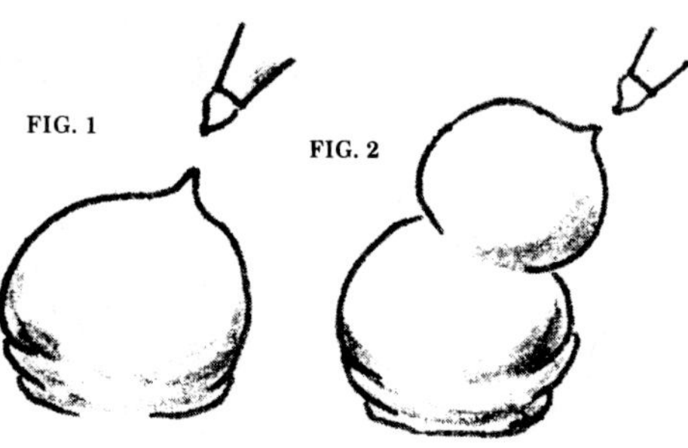

SIDE VIEW
Frog body and head

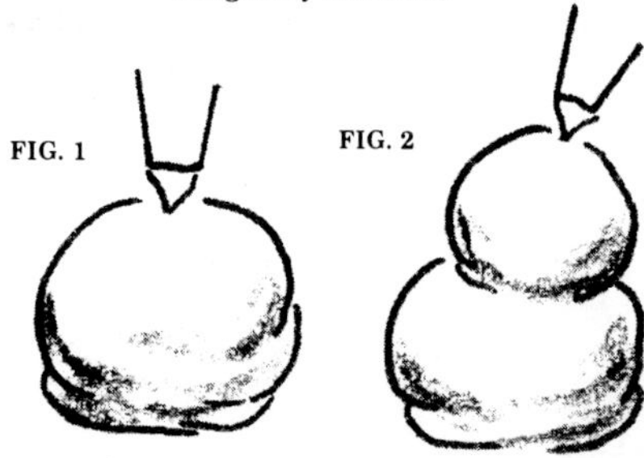

FRONT VIEW
Frog body and head

The main body "bubbles" should be piped with a tube with a ¼" cut tip or a #8 tip. The first bubble should form a solid base for the head bubble. The head bubble should be slightly offset to the front.

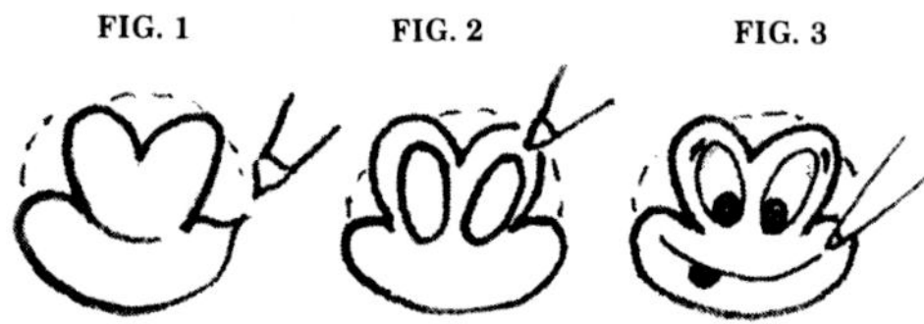

1) To detail the face we pipe two teardrop shaped bubbles to form the supports for the eyes. This is piped in green icing. Then bring a cylinder of icing around under the eyes to form the mouth area.

2) Pipe long oval shapes with white icing for the eyes.

3) With a small tube of black icing, using a #1 or smaller tip, pipe a smile line for the mouth, two dots for the eyes and two small lines for the eyebrows. Add a small red dot for a tongue.

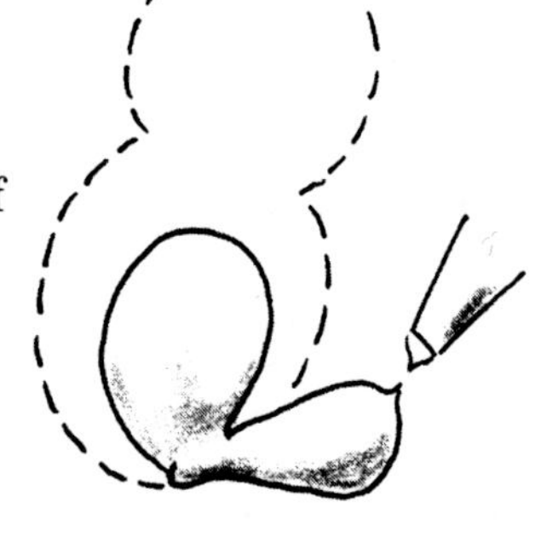

Detail of Legs:
The legs consist of two bubbles. One forms the upper leg and the other forms the foot.

4) Pipe two bubbles at the base of the body to indicate the front feet.

THE KITTEN!

What could be cuter than a little white kitten! Well, maybe a little tiger-striped kitten! Either way, a kitten makes an ideal cupcake design.

FIG. 1

Start with a round puff of icing for the head. Use a tip about the size of a #7.

FIG. 2

The body is a heavy "U" shape. Keep the neck thin. The back end should be a little heavier.

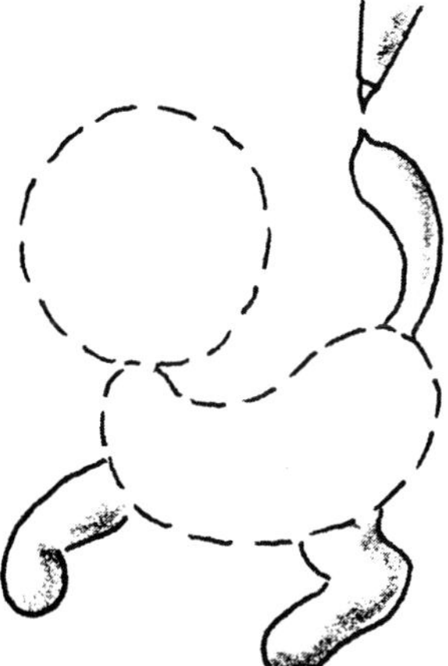

FIG. 3

With a #3 tip, pipe the front and rear right legs. Add the tail.

FIG. 4

Now with the same tube, add two pointed ears and the two left legs.
Then in white, add two small bubbles for the eyes. Add a few puffs of white icing for the chest.

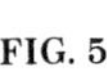

FIG. 5

Finish by drawing on the features of the face with a #1 or smaller black tube. Draw on the eyes, whiskers, eyebrows, and the mouthline.
If this design is done in white, you may want to outline the whole thing to bring out the detail.

NOTE:
You may want to add a colorful ball of yarn to brighten and add humor to the design.

Done in white, brown, or pastels, a cute little bunny cupcake for each guest will keep any children's party hoppin'. They're great for baby showers too!

FIG. 1   **SIDE VIEW**

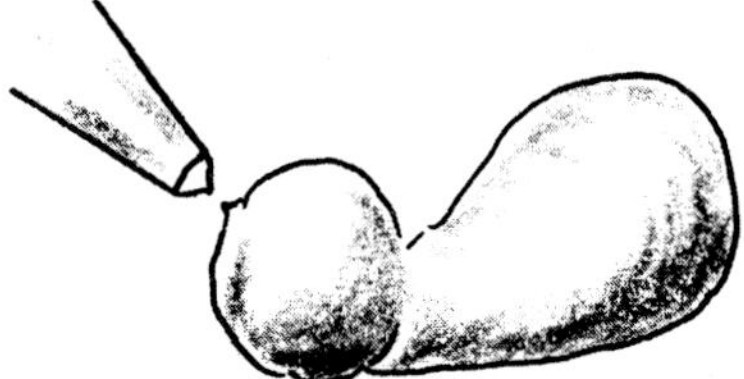

With a tube having a #7 or #8 tip, pipe the body and head. The body is an elongated bubble.

SIDE VIEW

FIG. 3

DETAIL OF LEGS, TAIL, EARS & NOSE

Pipe the ears in pink at the back of the head. Lay them onto the body for support and bring them out to a point. The front legs are small bubbles. The rear legs are made of a bubble for the upper leg and an elongated bubble for the foot. Pipe two small white bubbles for the eyes.

FIG. 2   **FRONT VIEW**

The head is a round bubble.

FIG. 4

Outline the pink ears in the color of the bunny. With a small black tube using a #1 or smaller, pipe the detail of the eyes, eyebrows, and a "W" shape for the mouth.

FIG. 5

A puff of white for the tail and a little pink or red nose are then added.

THE TURTLE!

Turtles may be noted for being slow, but as cupcake decorations, they are always winners.

FIG. 1   **TOP VIEW**

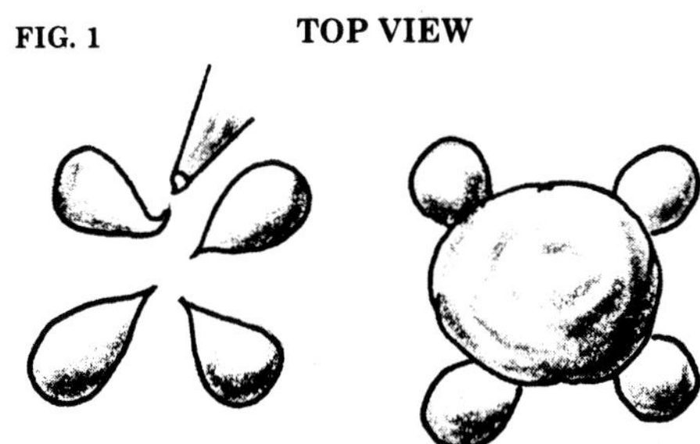

Pipe four teardrop shaped bubbles as shown. Use a #8 opening and light green icing. Next pipe a large bubble of darker green icing in the center of the four smaller bubbles.

FIG. 2   **SIDE VIEW**

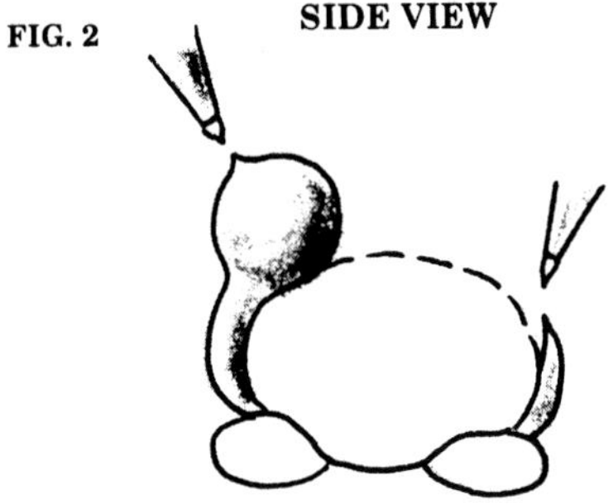

Next pipe the neck, head, and tail with the light green icing. Start the neck at the base of the shell bubble, then come up forming a ball on top for the head.

FIG. 3   **FRONT VIEW**

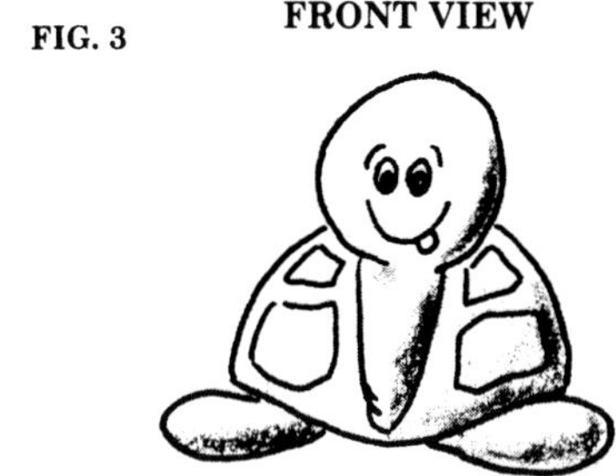

The features should be kept simple. Eyes, eyebrows, a smile, and a little red tongue. Pipe the features with a small tube cut to about a #1 or smaller.

FIG. 4

With a small black tube, draw segments on the shell as shown.

FIG. 5

A little black hat with a bright yellow flower adds color. Use a #3 tip for the hat. Just pipe a circle of icing around the head, then a bubble in the middle. Use a #1 tip for the flower.

Perhaps unlikely, but nevertheless, pigs are popular. Whether just a head or the whole pig, body and all, they make great cupcake decorations. They can be done in a pinkish-flesh tone or just plain pink.

FIG. 1

Begin with a round bubble piped with a #7 tube.

FIG. 2

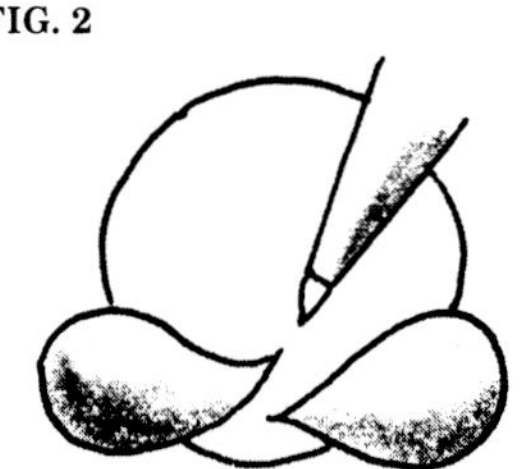

Add two teardrop shaped bubbles for the cheeks. Puff them bigger at the outside then bring them to the center.

FIG. 3

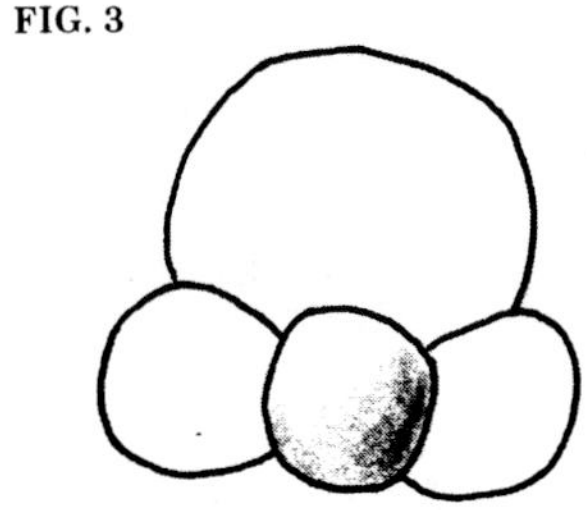

Next pipe a bubble for the nose between the two cheeks.

FIG. 4

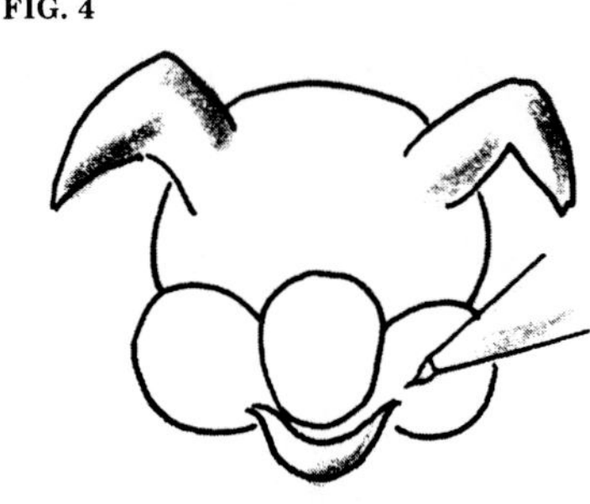

Bring a "U" shape under the nose to form a lower lip. Bring the ears out and down. Let off pressure to bring them to a point.

FIG. 5

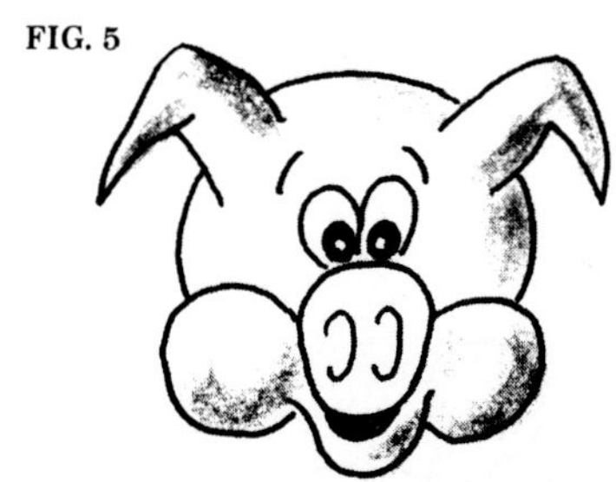

Finish by adding two small white puffs for the eyes. Then with a small black tube with approximately a #1 opening, pipe dots for the pupils of the eyes, two lines for the eyebrows, a smile line, and a little red dot for a tongue. The nostrils can be simply drawn on or pressed in with a sharp stick such as a meat skewer.

When doing the whole pig, we will use the same basic steps for the head as previously described only be sure to use tubes of appropriate sizes to ensure crisp detail. A #1 or even a #0 might be used for the black detail of the face.

FIG. 1

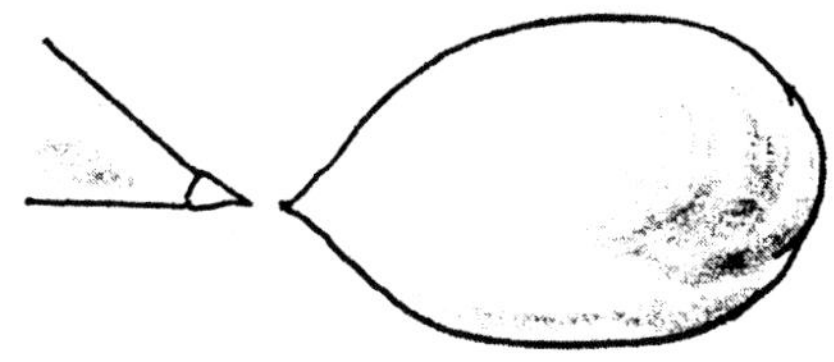

Start with a large, slightly elongated bubble for the body.

FIG. 2

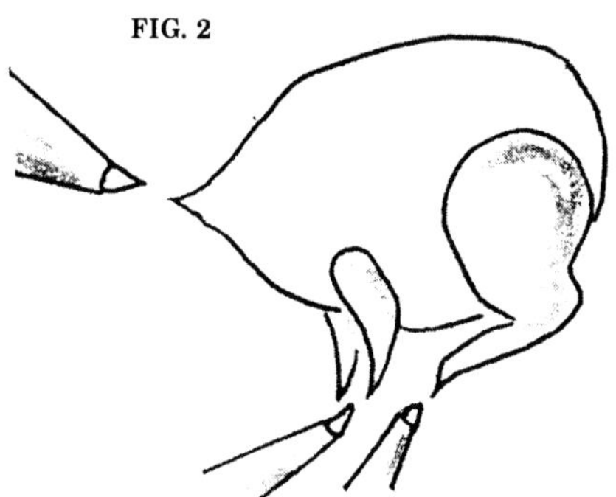

Add the legs. The back legs are simply bubbles for the "hams" then long teardrop shaped bubbles brought out for the lower legs.

FIG. 3

The front legs are just teardrop shaped bubbles. Add a little curly tail.

The facial expression

could be changed

for variation.

Well, we certainly don't want to find mice in the kitchen, that is unless they are made of icing! And as decorations for cupcakes, they are delightful! The top of the cupcakes might be iced in yellow to offer the idea of a piece of cheese. The mice should be piped in a fairly light shade of gray. Keeping the color light will keep the design crisp and allow the detail to show up vividly. Sliced almonds work perfectly for the ears. They add an accent of color, a delightful look of dimension, and they keep the design completely edible.

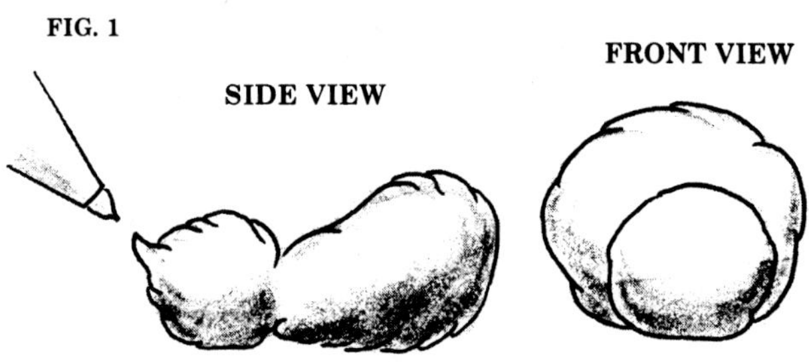

Pipe the bubbles for the body and head as shown. Hold the tube at about a 45° angle. Use a ¼" cut tip or a #8 tip.

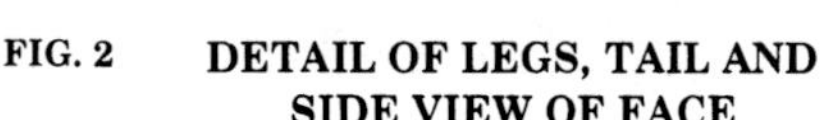

The back legs are simply two bubbles. The upper part should be somewhat oval in shape. The lower part is the foot. It should be a teardrop shaped bubble with the fullness at the toe. The front feet are two small bubbles of icing piped as shown. The tail should be piped with pink icing and can conform to whatever shape would best fit the space available.

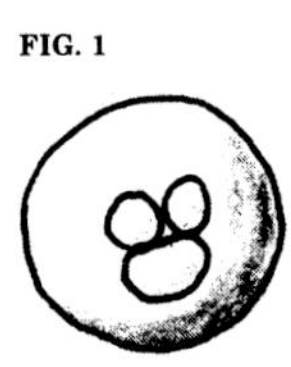
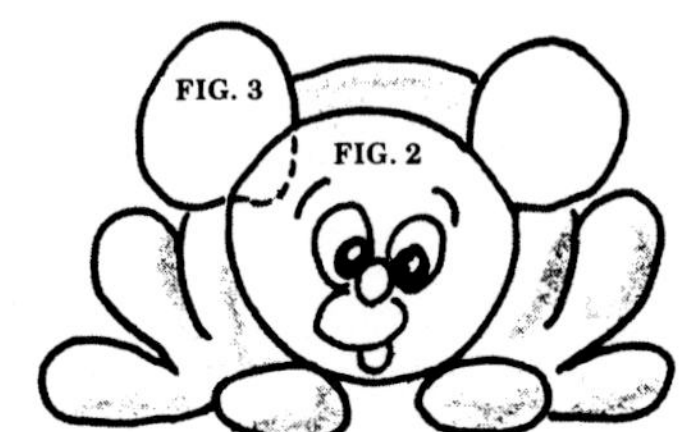

1) On the front of the "head" bubble, pipe three small bubbles of white icing as shown. Make the one in the middle a bit larger than the other two. These bubbles become the eyes and snout.

2) Using a small tube of black icing, pipe the detail of the face. Two dots for the eyes, a small bubble for the nose, and two small lines for eyebrows.

3) Insert two sliced almonds for the ears. Add a small red dot under the snout to indicate a tongue.

NOTE: If the mouse squeaks, oil it! (a little joke) HEH HEH!

This *"Big Cheese"* cake illustrates how these cupcake-sized mice can be used to decorate larger cakes.
To make this *"Wedge of Cheese"* cake, simply cut a quarter-sheet cake diagonally and stack.

     Make a round cake to resemble a lily pad and add a family of cute frogs. This cake is very popular.

Put a group of *"Crock-a-gators"* on a quarter sheet and you've got a sure winner!

Lions and tigers around a cake make a delightful creation. Add bears and you've got *"Lions and Tigers and Bears – Oh My"* –what a cute cake! Page 19

THE TEDDY BEAR FACE

The teddy bear is an ever-popular design. Whether it be for a child's birthday done in traditional brown tones or for a baby shower done in any number of pastel colors, teddy bears are always cute. Pink, blue, and yellow pastel shades are the most popular for shower cupcakes. This teddy bear can easily be adapted to become a panda bear.

FIG. 1 **SIDE VIEW**

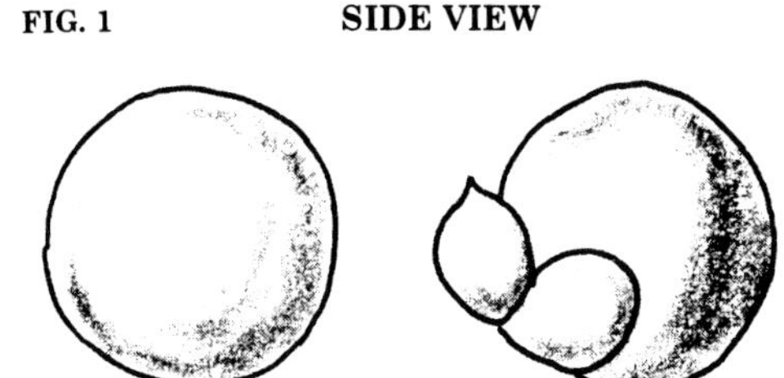

Pipe a round bubble for the head in brown or an appropriate pastel. Then pipe two teardrop shaped bubbles in white for the cheeks starting at the outside and coming toward the middle. Use a #7 tip or **cut** an equivalent size tip.

FIG. 2 **FRONT VIEW**

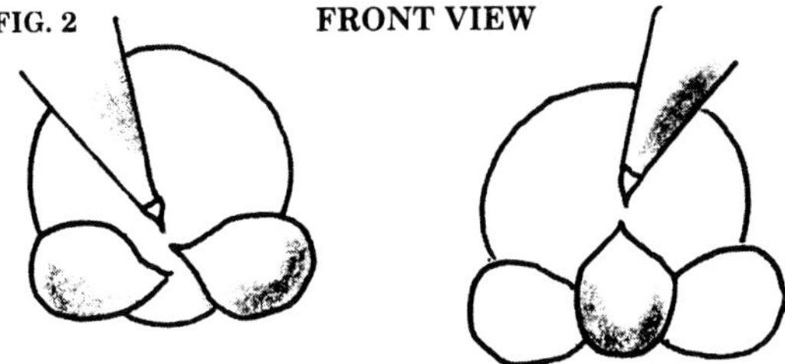

Then pipe the snout between the cheeks starting at the bottom and coming upward. The snout can be done in **white** or the same color as the head. Use a #7 size tip.

FIG. 3

FACE ADDITIONS

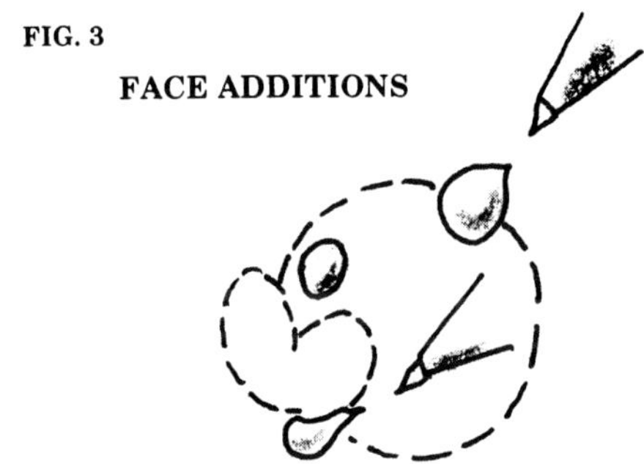

Pipe two white bubbles for the ears, two smaller bubbles for the eyes, and a "U" shape to indicate the lower lip.

FIG. 4 **FACE DETAIL**

Outline the white ears with the "head" color. Then with a small black tube add the nose, eyes, eyebrows, and a smile line. Finish with a little red tongue. Use a #0 size tip for the small detail.

Though the teddy bear face alone is very cute, adding a body offers variety and might be just right for those very special occasions. We would first do the face as previously described, only smaller. Because of the small size, care must be taken to keep the design crisp. Be sure to adjust tube sizes accordingly. Use a tube the size of a #5 for the body and a #00 for the face detail.

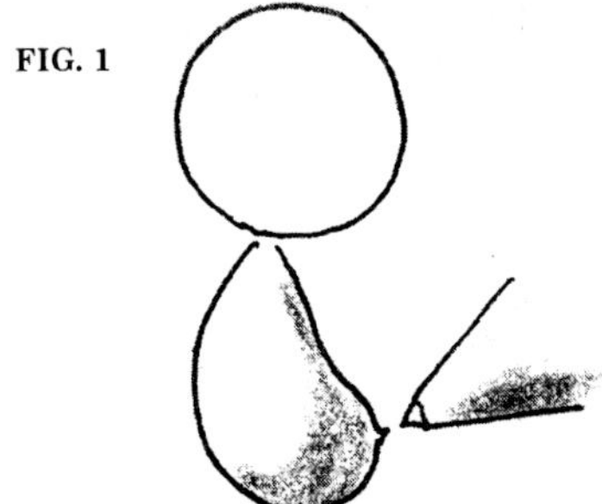

FIG. 1

The head should be made as previously described, only smaller. The body is a teardrop shaped bubble with a slight "C" shape to it. Keep it thin at the neck.

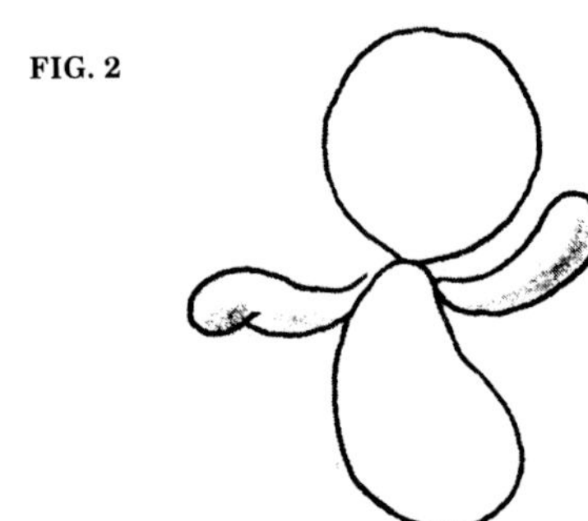

FIG. 2

The arms are long teardrops, heavier at the paws.

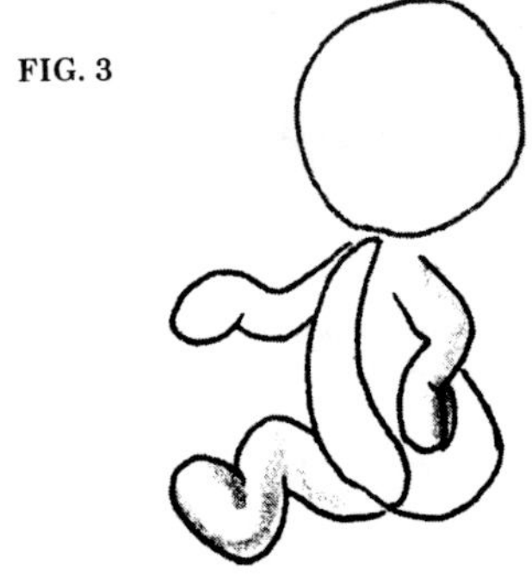

FIG. 3

This illustration shows the left arm in an optional position. The right leg should be piped next. Then a stripe of white down the front. This makes the design brighter.

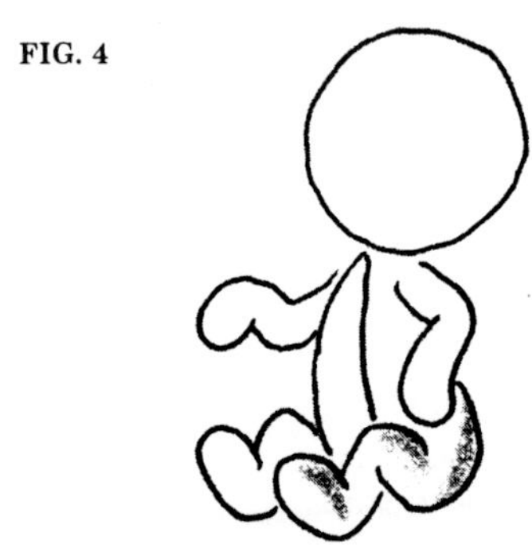

FIG. 4

Next pipe the other leg. Use enough pressure to make the legs full. Pipe a bubble for the foot.

NOTE: When doing the full figure of the Teddy Bear, use tubes of a size #5 for the head, body, arms, legs, etc., and a #0 or smaller for the black detail.

NOTE: You might add a colorful shirt to change the style or add variety to your cupcakes.

THE LION AND TIGER FACES

These two designs are so similar they can both be described at the same time with only minor variations. Both of these faces are extremely popular. They are so cute they just seem to "jump" at the viewer. Both are about the same color, shape, and size. The color should be a golden yellow. These designs should be piped with a tip the size of a #8 for the large bubbles and a #1 or smaller size tip for the detail. Note: to mix a golden yellow icing, start with bright lemon yellow, add a small amount of red and a tiny amount of blue.

FIG. 1 **¾ VIEW**

First pipe the large bubble of the head with golden yellow icing. Next pipe the two cheek bubbles in white icing. They should be side by side, to the front of the first bubble.

FIG. 2 **FRONT VIEW**

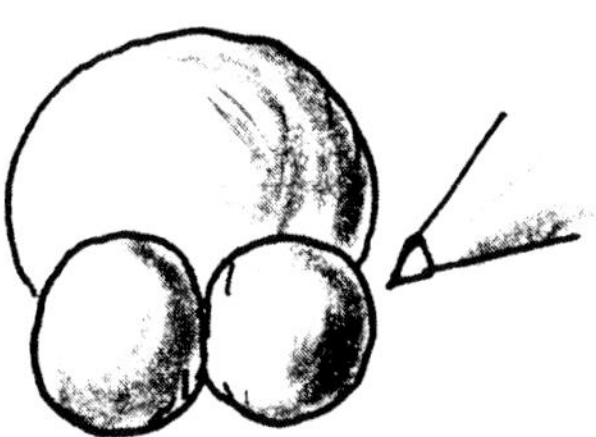

Be sure to pipe all three of these basic bubbles as **round** balls!

ADDITIONS TO FACE

FIG. 3

Pipe two round bubbles in white at the top of the head as shown and two more a bit smaller for the eyes. Then pipe a little pointed puff for the beard, also in white. The nose should be a long cylinder shape a bit larger at the end. This should be piped in the yellow color.

DETAIL OF FACE

FIG. 4

The details of the face should be piped with a small black tube. For the tiger, outline the white ears with a golden yellow and then with a line of black. Add two dots for the eyes and two small lines for the eyebrows. Add a black tip to the end of the nose, three black dots on each cheek for the whiskers, and outline the mouth. Add a little red dot for the tongue. Add black stripes on the head as shown.

For the lion, eliminate the stripes and add a mane. For the color, use a mixture of golden yellow, brown, and white marbled together. Pipe the mane with a star tip.

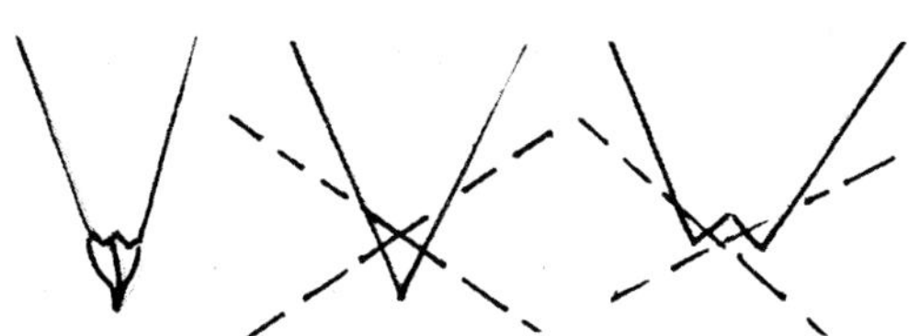

A star tip can be cut as shown. Be sure to keep all sides even. I prefer a cut star, but a #16 would work.

As a cupcake decoration, a horse head is very popular. It seems almost every young girl wants to own a horse, and though a cupcake is certainly not a horse, it serves as a delightful substitute at the birthday party. Fun and quick, horse head cupcakes are perfect for young horse fanciers. The most popular colors for horses are brown, black, gray, and gold. Be sure to use a different color or shade of color for the mane. For example, if we have a dark brown horse, the mane might be a lighter shade or a marbled shade. This creates contrast and adds to the overall attractiveness of the design.

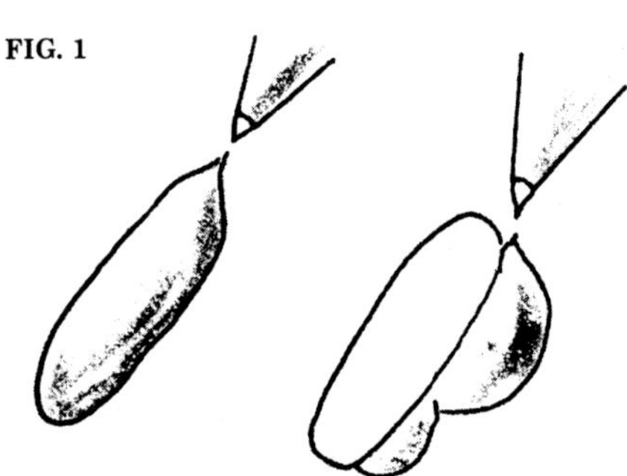

The face of a horse is basically flat to the front, so start by piping a straight cylinder shape at about a 45° angle as shown. A #8 tip is about the right size. Then pipe two half bubbles under the cylinder, one small one to indicate the lower lip or chin and one larger one to indicate the jaw bone.

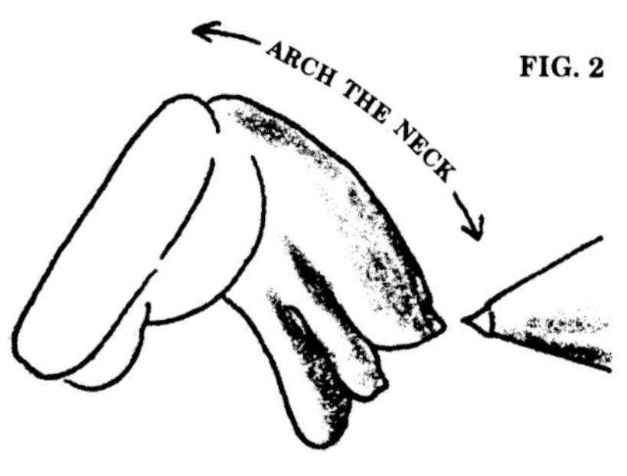

Next, add the neck. It may be necessary to pipe the neck in two or three strokes. Keep them smooth and slightly arched.

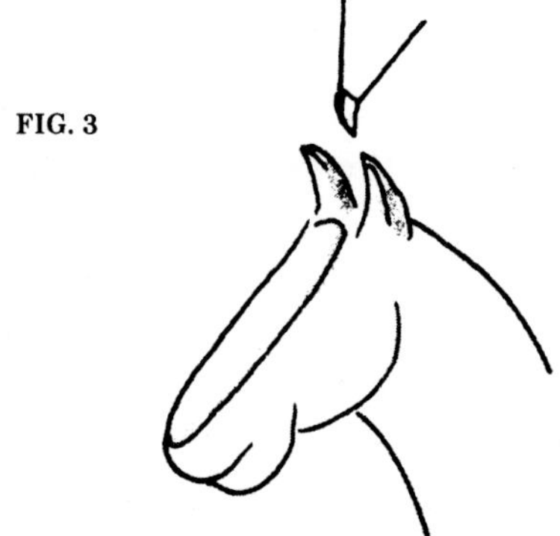

Bring out two pointed bubbles for ears. Add a white stripe or "blaze" to the face. This brightens the design and adds color.

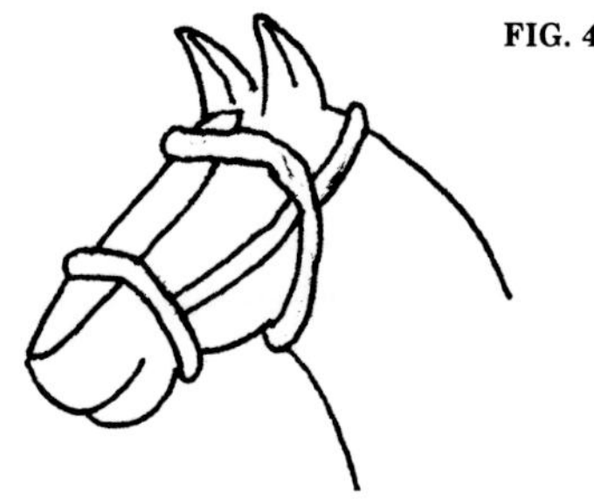

With a bright color such as yellow, red, silver, green, etc., add a halter as shown. Use a #3 tip for this.

With a small black tube, draw on the eye and nostril. Add the mane with a cut star tube or a #16 tip. Marble in different shades of color to add contrast. Make the mane long and flowing. This will help cover any "seams" in the neck. To finish, add the reins.

THE CROC-A-GATOR

This ferocious design is the hit of any party. It is created using a tube striped with yellow icing then filled with green icing. See "the frog". The tip should be cut to ¼", or use a #7 tip. It is piped using a technique called pressure control. That is, we must control the pressure with which we squeeze the decorating bag in order to achieve the elongated body necessary. Also, to achieve the texture, (slightly ruffled), we want to shake the tube slightly in an "in and out" motion as we pipe the body.

TOP VIEW

FIG. 1

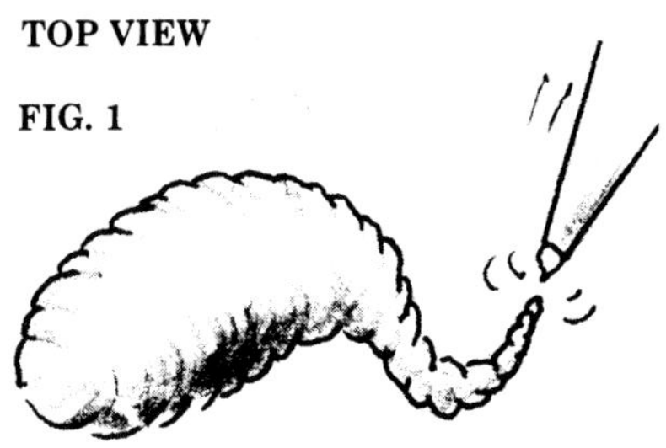

Pipe the body first. Start from the front with more pressure and gradually lessen pressure as you work to the tail. Remember to jiggle the tube slightly to make the bumpy texture.

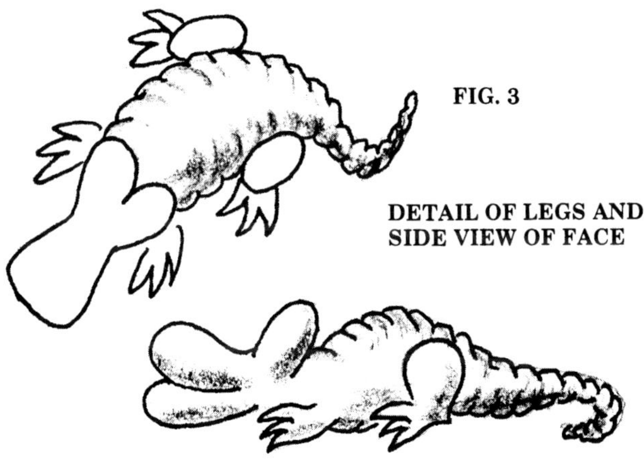

FIG. 3

DETAIL OF LEGS AND SIDE VIEW OF FACE

The back legs are made with a bubble for the top part. Then bring out three pointed toes. On the front, bring out three toes from under the front of the body as shown.

FIG. 2   **FRONT VIEW**

Pipe the head (face) by making two teardrop shaped bubbles to support the eyes, then two long teardrop shapes for the nose - one on the bottom then one right on top of it. Make these bubbles larger at the front.

DETAIL OF THE FACE
1) SIDE   2) FRONT

1) With a small tube of white icing, pipe oval shapes for the eyes and several white pointed teeth.

2) Then with a small black tube, pipe in two dots for the eyes, two small lines for eyebrows and two little "C" shapes to indicate nostrils. Add a small red tongue. Use a #1 or smaller size tip for the detail.

You're not barking up the wrong tree with this cute K-9 design. This hound dog cup cake top is a sure winner!

FIG. 1

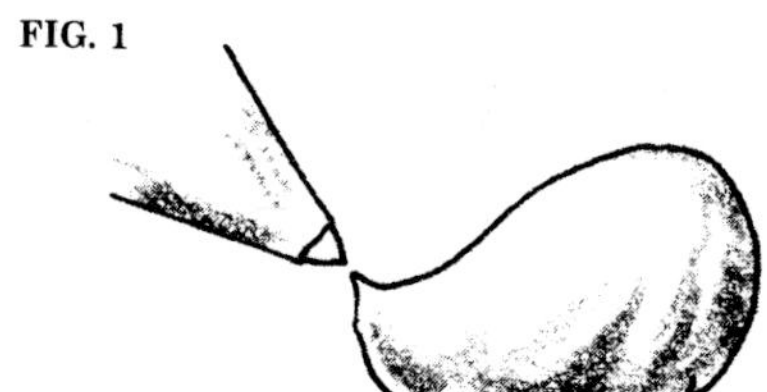

Start with the body using a tan or light brown color. Pipe an elongated bubble. Begin with heavier pressure then taper down to form a large teardrop shape. Use a #8 size tip.

FIG. 2

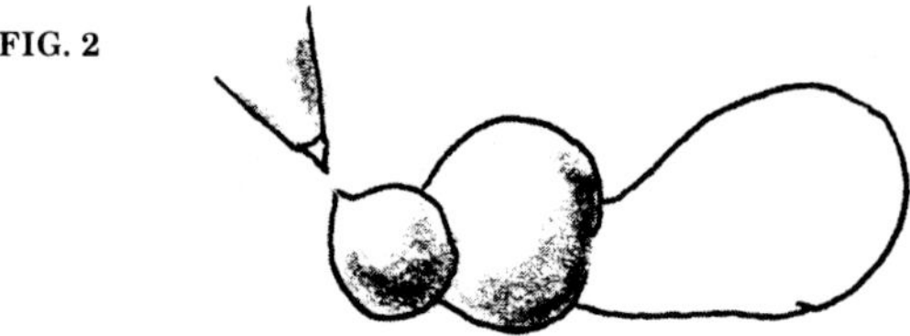

Next add the head and cheeks. These are just round bubbles.

FIG. 3

FRONT VIEW

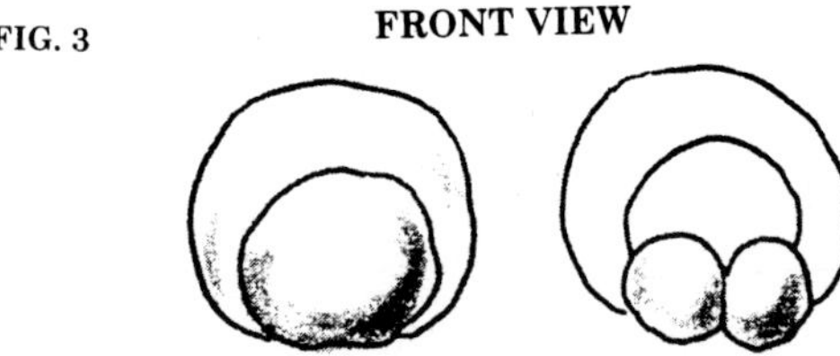

The cheeks are **white** round bubbles placed side by side.

FIG. 4

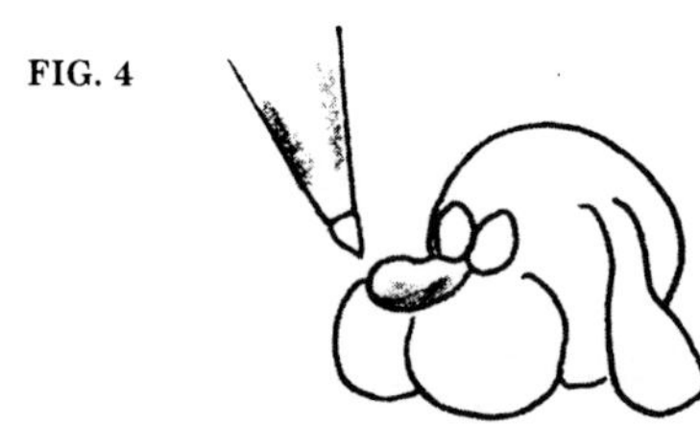

Add the nose line between the two cheeks. It should be the same color as the rest of the dog. Use a #3 tip.

FIG. 5

The rear legs are formed with a rounded bubble for the upper part and a cylinder shape for the lower leg. The front legs are cylinders of icing brought around to the sides of the face from the shoulder area.

The ears are long teardrop shapes. The nose is a round bubble of black icing. The tail is a long cylinder of icing done in black or the color of the dog. Bring it around in a shape that best fills the available space.

Add two small white bubbles for the eyes.

FIG. 6

Finish by adding the black detail with a #1, or smaller, tube. Detail the eyes as shown. Add three small black dots on each cheek for whiskers and a "w" shaped line to indicate the mouth. Add a pink tongue and a top knot of hair (optional). Use a #16, cr smaller, tube for the hair.

Another great design. Simple, quick, a delight to young and old alike. Especially appropriate on banana cupcakes.

FIG. 1

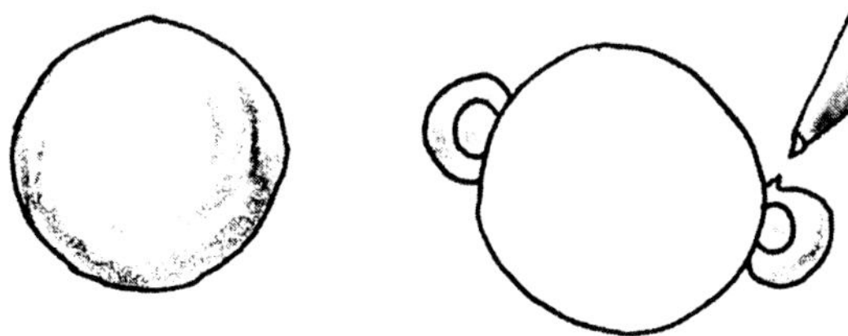

Start with a round bubble for the head. This should be a light brown color. Then, with a flesh tone, add two small bubbles for ears and outline them with the same tube.

FIG. 3

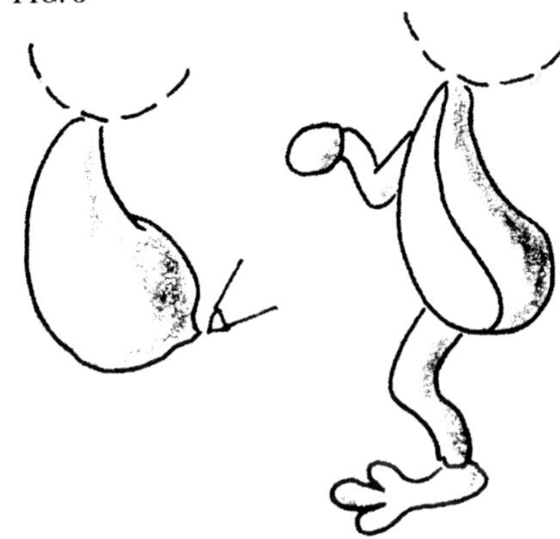

Pipe a pear shape for the body. Add the right arm and leg with the brown. Pipe a stripe of white down the front to add color. With flesh color, pipe a bubble for the hand then add the foot. Bring out three small bubbles to in dicate toes.

FIG. 2

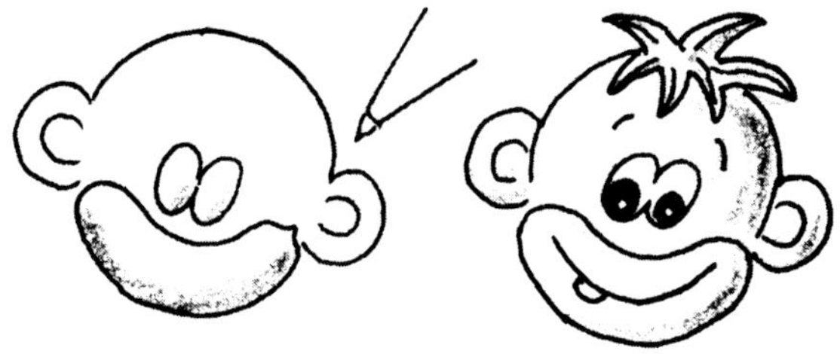

With the flesh tone, bring a wide "U" shape around for the mouth area. Add two white dots for the eyes. Finish by detailing with a small black tube. Draw on the eyebrows, mouth line and two dots for the eyes. Add a small red dot for the tongue. Add some hair with a #16 star or cut star tube. Marble light and dark brown together for the hair color.

FIG. 4

Pipe a yellow banana across the hand then add three fingers and a thumb using small bubbles of flesh color. Add the second leg, foot, arm, and hand as shown.

NOTE: The tail can be piped on, or a piece of shoe string licorice can be used.

BUTTERCREAM ICING...

Many decorators have a particular formula or recipe for buttercream icing they find preferable as to flavor or consistency - and there is certainly room for some latitude in the icing you might use to create the designs illustrated in this book. However, because these designs are, for the most part, quite dimensional, it is necessary to use an icing that is **firm** enough to hold its shape. The following is a recipe for a simple buttercream icing that works very well for this type of decorating. This is a 2 to 1 formula. That is, twice as much sugar as shortening.

FOR 20 QT. MIXER

12½ lbs. sugar (powdered)
6¼ lbs. shortening (Sweetex or Crisco)
1¾ lbs. water
1½ oz. salt
2½ oz. vanilla

SMALL RECIPE

2 lbs. powdered sugar
2 cups shortening (Sweetex or Crisco)
⅓ cup water
¼ - ½ tsp. salt
2 tsp. vanilla

Mix sugar, water, 25% of the shortening, salt, and vanilla until smooth . . . about 5 minutes at low speed.

Add the remaining shortening, mix about 5 more minutes at low speed.

Scrape down and mix for 3-5 more minutes at 2nd speed.

As a flavor enhancer, add about 10% Bright White, Royal White, or similar emulsifier to the second mix. The 10% is based on the shortening amount.

To make a smaller batch, simply cut the ingredient amounts in half.

This full-size cake sculpture replica of the *"Real Life Midgets"* with Ringling Bros. Circus was created by Roland A. Winbeckler for their wedding.

This cute little leprechaun is an example of the work done in Roland A. Winbeckler's cake-sculpture class.